Serendipity

Nancy Viera

Copyright © 2023 Nancy Viera

De Colores Publishing, Denver CO, 2023

All rights reserved.

For Monte

"And I'd give up forever to touch you
'Cause I know that you feel me somehow"
Iris by The Goo Goo Dolls

Also by Nancy Viera

The Grief and The Happiness
Silhouette
Chicago and You

Serendipity

HERE I LAND

You're here
eye to eye
Lips to lips
Your hand lands on my hip
Like it's home
You drop a kiss on my forehead and I know it's home
You touch my face and it casts a spell
We are here by kismet
I'd hop on a million more planes to land here again with you
Your brown eyes hold my soul and even if wanted to I can't
look away
I don't want to look away
I want to be here in the in between of everything
In between cities
In between the sheets
In between glances
in between your stories
and the way you make me laugh
In between is this real or just a dream
You tore down the armor I didn't know I had so effortlessly
All you did was call out my name
I have nothing to hide with you
Your arms are the place I want to land on every time
Lets make this last and get lost in the sky together

PRAYER

I don't have to wait in benches anymore
He doesn't make me beg
Or cry
He turns on the senses that laid dormant for years
He's the type of man you read in books
Immortalized in the pages and stories
The type you pray for
If I was a writer I'd write poems about the way he loves
The way I love him
The way the heavens would speak of him
He is gospel on my skin
There is only love in his absolution
Raise me to the sky
Amen, amen, amen
I will worship his sins
Amen

FLY WITH ME

The man from seat 11E
Flight 403
Depart 9:45
DEN
LAX
No carry on
Just my heart
Just his beat
Mixing
Drifting flying
Falling in love
The man from seat 11E
Takes my hand
Meets me in Las Vegas
Everything happened
Nothing stayed there

Nancy Viera

GOOD MORNING

Now that I know the way your
Lips feel on mine I know
What is like to miss you
You linger on my skin
Come back to bed
Stay with me
I promise not to wake you with false promises
One day was not enough and yet I remember every way you
made my core shake
I'm this close to saying something
But
I'll wait
Maybe next time
When you stay

Nancy Viera

KISMET

Maybe tomorrow
  Maybe next year
  The time does not matter
  The spell is casted
  I can't seem to comeback to myself
  It's like the piece of my heart I protected the most was stolen
  Except I'm not scared
  Because I think you stole it
  I think you're mixing it
  In cauldrons of dreams
  Adventure and love
  Sweet serendipity
  I think tomorrow you'll be sweeping off my feet taking me with you
  Maybe tomorrow
  I am counting to ten fighting back fears
  Until tomorrow

Nancy Viera

SWEEPING LOVE

Do you believe in fate now?
Now that you are standing feet away from me
Now that the tension slowly fades
There is an enormous amount of desire cursing through my heart
Wielding its power and love directly into yours
I long for us to crash through the surface
and reach moments of bliss yet undiscovered
How deep can we go?
If I slip will you catch me?

Nancy Viera

DANCE WITH ME

You held my hand yesterday at the party
You wrapped your strong arms around me
You didn't keep me a secret
You empowered me with your love
With the tender way you pay attention
Hold the door
Tell me to wait
I'd wait many lifetimes again to see you
Should you forget me in this one
I'll be at the cliff of the next time we meet
I'll remind you of the beat between your chest and mine
How your fingers run down the curve of my neck down to my breast
I'll bring back the quiet of the morning
To welcome you back again
Inside the deepest part
The part where you held me
When time stopped

Nancy Viera

ONE DAY

Does this happen often to you?
Do you fall in love in one day?
Do you believe the universe conspired to have us meet?
I'll stop asking questions eventually
When my mind believes my heart
When it stops feeling like a dream
We've dived into this portal might as well sink into its depths
and find out what waits at the other end
Hold my hand
Here we go
Fall with me

LJO

He is familiar
Tall with a smile full of life
He is life
A voice gentle baritone with melodies hugging cities
He is home
Accent and swag from the bay
Where the most beautiful beats follow him
He loves deep and sweet
Just like his kisses
He was a stranger
But in between tequila fueled talks
He let me in
He told me the sweet spot
The place that makes him happy
The life he has chosen full of tales and adventures
No regrets
There's nothing fickle about him
I'll never forget the way he lingers
He needs no introduction
He's simply the one
My muse

Serendipity

GENTLE

No one sees me naked
Not the way you did
With your eyes looking directly at mine
With your soul meeting mine and going for a dance
I want to love you endlessly
Undress my fears with your laugh
Oh, I love the way you make me laugh

YOU AND ME

A love with no witnesses
A private escape
From the wars inside our hearts
Just you
Just me
Just our essence
Dancing
Mingling
Embarking on a unknown journey
Only strangers can take

Nancy Viera

PLEASURE

I feel hungry
I want to ravish the very skin that fits inside me so perfectly
Run my mouth up and down
While your eyes steal my soul
Let my throat be the very place you release your worries and your tension
Come as you are
I want the delicious elixir to fill me
and find the cure that seals every inch of scars left behind from others before you
You lay flowers at my feet and honor every inch of me
Let me honor now every breath you take
as I hold my breath to bring you pleasure

WHISPERS OF STORIES

I dream
   in slow motion of all the stories untold
Of
The valleys that hide the bodies
One more goes missing the world stops
Listens then moves on
Mounds full of secrets
The secrets you keep
I find the stories as I peel off
Layers
And layers
And layers
I am of many colors
i am of many names
Ardent nights wait for me to arrive and fill the flower pots with whispers
Tell me your story
Every time I think I know everything the red valley opens above me and shows me the screech of the eagle sliding and soaring spreading the stories of those before me
Heaven rains wisdom on me
My grandmother whispers her recipe and I'm left with blankets and heaps of responsibility
"Tell our stories hija mía
Roar when you speak of me, "she says
She's lived behind a wall but that wall never stopped her. It won't stop any of us.
I am not the mother forgotten next to her gas stove frying the beans rolling the tortillas filled of her dreams
But I am her biggest dreams

Serendipity

I've never had a father love me but I imagine it feels like something magnetic
Like a hug from the sky that shrinks your worries
He was allowed to walk away, my mother would never
I braid my story with my mothers hoping the ending is sealed with blessings from her mother
The endless river cries for my story
Will it be full of sorrow too, will it bring her joy
Please river don't take them away, keep them safe
These stories
Will they turn my bones to syrup
Will I move in tears away from tears
There are birds in my mouth screeching for forgiveness
Who are you to silence them
All I want is the warmth of your refuge
Accept me and cradle me in between the stories that you accept without colors
My story is enough and untold no more

Nancy Viera

GALAXY

No, I will not go with you to the end of this galaxy
    You've promised to swallow the very beautiful poison that took you away from
    your hopes and dreams
    Yet
    You sit with her and cradle her heart while she owns and chews your brain
    You promised safe haven to a million stars
    And burned them with love and might
    Don't ask me to loop universes and dreams with ribbons of satin blood
    When you cut them with the sharp of your tongue
    Leave me alone
    Let me sit here on my star
    While I burn alone

Nancy Viera

SLOW BURN

I've made a mistake
    I've fallen for him
    I've fallen for the unspoken promise
    The silence in between his eyes
    The ones that are beautiful pools of ferocious gold
    The ones that drown me with their shimmer
    The gentle gracing of his hand next to mine when we walk
    It's electric
    It's too soon
    Too quick
    It's not a mistake
    But I'm afraid
    Will this be like before
    Quick and painful
    Or will it be a slow burn

Nancy Viera

DEMONS

I do not know how to
    Blur the lines in between
    Your existence and mine
    They beg
    And I,
    Suffer
    I wonder
    If the reasons that scare you to touch the surface
    Have anything to do with me
    Will those demons clawing at your heart ease out
    Fade away
    Just long enough for you to reach for my hand
    Some can blur the lines
    Together
    Are you my savior?

Nancy Viera

THE ARTIST

I wish I could dress the shivers
    Brought on by his touch
    The pure, the kind
    I'd love myself in the deep
    Of his ocean eyes
    Should he cross the sky again
    March right into my embrace
    Of a million kisses
    I never want it to stop
    I want my body to be the music of his paint brush
    Dancing to me
    Making me his art
    I am his art

MI MADRE

Esta va por el tronco que me vio nacer
Por la poderosa historia de mujer que entre tormentas y desvelos
Hace que sus hijas vuelen alto
Alto asta donde no las alcanza el viento
de las palabras que quieran herirlas
Alto donde la luz que les dió brilla con su resplandor
El resplandor que les molesta a esos que no saben admirar lo que es
La guerra de llevar en sus hombros la carga sola
y aún llevar la ternura de una rosa
sus cicatrices invisibles llenas de historias que nunca contará
Que dieras tú por tener el brillo reluciente
y el valor para salir al mundo
Al mundo que te juzga asta el color de tus ojos
y lo largo de tus metas
No la conoces
Y no tendrás el privilegio de ser testigo de sus poderes y su habilidad de mover el mundo con una sonrisa y sus palabras
Ella es mi madre
Ella es libre
Y tu?

PANDEMIC PAIN

Nothing is happening to me
   around me
   The vortex
   Of this snowstorm
   hugs my tormented soul
   Trapped inside myself
   Longing for air
   Longing for freedom
   My lungs are on fire
   The cool of his touch would be my only saving grace

I can't breath

Its because nothing is happening around me

DOMINGO

No me quiero alistar solo los domingos
    A que me lleves a comer
    A que me lleves a los lugares donde solo tú felicidad baila
    No quiero quedarme callada mientras sirvo tu plato
    Mientras me cubro esa marca
    Que con flores se perdonó
    No quiero verte sonriendo
    Porque cuando me vez feliz a mi
    te enojas
    No quiero ser tu todo
    Tu sirviente
    Tu amante de vez en cuando
    Quiero ser yo
    Y voy hacer
    Lo que se me de mi gana

WILD WAVES

Waves of music flat through my veins
    They will fill my soul
    With the healing
    Of every grain of sand
    Deep in the hollow of my heart
    The emerald of my desires
    There you are
    There you are

DANCE WITH ME

The moonlight dances
   Around my blue dress
   The rouge of my lips
   Flirts with the flames of the fire
   Deep inside me
   Shall we dance?

GLITTER OF SUNSHINE

Lifting you up
    From the ambers of the fire
    From the ash
    The playground is now safe
    You are allowed to be here
    To be pink
    You are allowed to be the yellow
    You are allowed to make everything glitter
    You are allowed to sing
    The song of your heart

DIVINE ROSE

Fields of dreams
    Running towards me
    I get to be here
    Taking up space
    Nourishing the earth
    Healing the ground
    I get to dive into the divine
    I get to dance and blossom
    Into the rose I am
    I am divine

COMUNITY

FISTS OF MUSIC
   SHIFTING THE WAVE
   FILLING THE HOLLOW OF MY HEART
   LET IT RAIN LOVE
   BLOOM FROM THE SWEET MELODY
   FILL THE CAVE YOU HIDE IN WITH LIGHT
   FALL INTO MY ARMS
   YOU ARE SAFE
   YOU HAVE ARRIVED
   YOU ARE LOVED

Nancy Viera

Nancy Viera is a Mexican American writer. She is the author of a memoir, The Grief and The Happiness, and has written two poetry collections, Silhouette and Chicago and You. She is the host of City Silhouettes, a local artist showcase and belongs to the Colorado Poets Center. Nancy writes both in English and Spanish. Her work has been showcased at the Denver Art Museum.

    Follow for more on Instagram @Omgnancita
        Www.nancymviera.com
    Portrait by Ashley Reed

Nancy Viera

www.ingramcontent.com/pod-product-compliance
Lightning Source LLC
LaVergne TN
LVHW031614060526
838201LV00065B/4840